PROBLEM SOLVED

THE LEADER'S GUIDE TO IDENTIFYING SYMPTOMS, MAKING A DIAGNOSIS, AND WRITING A CURABLE PLAN.

Drs. Darryl & Lawanne' Grant

Copyright © 2019
Darryl L. Grant & Lawanne' S. Grant

Book Package and Publication:
Leadership DevelopME, LLC: www.leadershipdevelopme.com

All rights reserved. No part of this book may be used or reproduced by any means, graphic, electronic, or mechanical, including photocopying, recording, taping or by any information storage retrieval system without the written permission of the publisher except in the case of brief quotations embodied in critical articles and reviews.

Books may be ordered through booksellers or by contacting:

Leadership DevelopME, LLC
Website: www.leadershipdevelopme.com

Because of the dynamic nature of the Internet, any web addresses or links contained in this book may have changed since publication and may no longer be valid. The views expressed in this work are solely those of the author and do not necessarily reflect the views of the publisher, and the publisher hereby disclaims any responsibility for them.

Any people depicted in stock imagery provided by Thinkstock are models, and such images are being used for illustrative purposes only. Certain stock imagery © Thinkstock.

ISBN: 978-0-359-78026-6
Library of Congress Control Number: 2019943302

Printed in the United States of America

Dedication

This book is dedicated to those who are committed to the process of discovering the solution to problems.

Table of Contents

Introduction 1

Step 1: Acknowledge the Problem 5

Step 2: Make an Appointment 11

Step 3: Identify the Symptoms 15

Step 4: Give a Diagnosis 21

Step 5: Prescribe the Plan 29

Step 6: Schedule Follow-Ups 37

Step 7: Adjust the Prescription 45

Step 8: Make a Referral to the Specialist 53

Conclusion 61

About the Authors 64-67

    Dr. Darryl L. Grant 64

    Dr. Lawanne' S. Grant 66

References 68

Introduction

The United States Census Bureau (2011) reports that 30% of the population has earned a bachelor's degree or higher. Only 2% of this sub-population hold doctorate degrees. Many consider the 2% to be extremely brilliant or adept individuals who are acutely proficient in everything they do. This is far from the reality of those who make up the 2%. The truth is, we don't have all of the answers, we're not versed in every subject, and there's no mental database that taps into the absolute solution for worldwide epidemics.

We share this misnomer because we've discovered that those in the 2% are considered scholars only because they've demonstrated the commitment and discipline to discover the truth, using a theoretical and research-based approach. This is true in medicine, education, business, and other recognized fields of study.

Just in case you're a part of the 2% we're discussing, please don't become offended by our admission. We're a part of the 2% as well.

However, it's our strong belief that leaders, regardless of educational ranking, should be fully convinced of their ability to solve problems. This will require leaders to admit what they don't know, so that they can begin the journey of discovering what they should know.

Although we studied at different universities, with one concentrating on leadership and the church and the other, leadership and business, the common message received from our professors was that the world would expect us to be experts once those three letters landed behind our names. One professor explained it best, saying that people would come to us just as they go to medical doctors when there's a problem in their bodies. Hence, we must have the knowledge to perform organizational diagnoses, whatever your "organization" might be, and develop strategies that produce measurable remedies.

This vivid word picture made a lasting impression that sharpened our approach to solving problems. In this book, we will share eight manageable steps that will help you identify, assess, and develop a plausible plan for problems that you are facing or will encounter in the future.

Before you take the first step, remember the analogy of solving problems using the medical doctor's routine approach. Put on your lab coat, grab a pen, keep lots of paper or your laptop nearby. You are getting ready to become a recognized doctor in the field of problem-solving.

Step 1: Acknowledge the Problem

Have you ever met someone who had obvious signs of illness but refused to take any medication? Or even worse, the person who's fully aware that disease is ravaging their health but keeps this devastating secret to themselves? This stubborn and self-serving response only gives permission for the condition to escalate from one level to another. The only way to address the infirmity is to admit there is a problem and seek help immediately.

As you take a microscopic look at the problem at hand, the first step is to acknowledge that *a* problem persists. Good leaders never turn their face away from challenges; rather, they give full attention to resolving the issue. When you ignore a lingering cough, it has the potential to turn into a more serious case of the flu that can eventually lead to pneumonia if not treated in a timely manner. This domino effect happens in the same way when a leader ignores problems from the greatest to the least.

We've discovered that most leaders ignore problems for the following reasons:

1. Lack of self-confidence to handle conflict.
2. The necessity to identify the people contributing to the problem.
3. Fear of losing team members.
4. The requirement to make hard decisions.
5. The mandate to change processes or upgrade systems.

This list is not exhaustive and perhaps your reason for ignoring problems is not on the list. Nevertheless, it's important that you make a commitment to get past negative perceptions of your leadership ability by tapping into the courageous leader within you. Failing to acknowledge the problem at hand, will set the stage, allowing the dilemma to overtake and suffocate your productive efforts.

Leaders who ignore activity that works against their vision qualify among those who use a laissez-faire leadership style. This type of leader takes a "hands-off" approach, believing that everything will eventually work out if they don't interfere. The results of laissez-faire leadership are often chaotic because the leader essentially leaves the chips to fall where they may, rather than guiding the direction of the chips to ensure that they land in their proper places.

Remember, leaders are called to use their influence to guide an individual or group toward an expected end. While you by no means should micromanage every minute detail, (that's a sign of poor delegation), you should be aware of the processes that team members are expected to follow. When there is activity or behavior that impedes productivity and causes a malfunction, the leader shouldn't be afraid to acknowledge the problem at hand.

Leadership Nugget: Problems are not a sign of weak leadership; they are opportunities to demonstrate the leader's strength to redirect, correct, and implement strategies that lead to positive outcomes.

SOLVE THE PROBLEM

What holds you back from acknowledging problems when you see them?

What will you do to overcome barriers that cause you to hesitate or ignore your responsibility to acknowledge problems?

Make a list of the problems you currently observe within your organization or team:

1.	6.
2.	7.
3.	8.
4.	9.
5.	10.

Why is it important for you to acknowledge the problems you listed?

_____
_____
_____
_____
_____
_____
_____
_____
_____
_____
_____
_____

Step 2: Make an Appointment

Imagine being at home with a terrible headache. Whether you want to admit it or not, the continued and forceful throbbing has forced you to acknowledge your discomfort. Furthermore, it's clear that the pain won't be relieved with just a few hours of rest or a quiet hour. Considering these variables, you accept the fact that you'll have to schedule the time needed to either purchase an over-the-counter antidote or make an appointment with your doctor at your first opportunity.

Now that you've acknowledged the problem, the next step requires that you make an appointment. The responsibilities of leadership are never-ending. As long as people are following you, you will always have questions to answer, job descriptions to define, and inspired vision to share. Your fiscal responsibilities will never disappear and your obligation to create sustainability will be a constant. For this reason, it's important that you schedule focused time to search for the best solution.

Problems deliberately avoid making appointments with solutions. Why? Because solutions expose, uncover, and halt the poor habits caused by problems. Hence, solutions should initiate the unwanted meeting with problems. Leaders are expected to have answers or access to resources that yield them. Therefore, it's important that you schedule designated time whereby solutions and problems are forced to meet head on.

Once you acknowledge that there is a problem, determine when you will conduct one or a combination of the following:

1. Focus Groups
2. Interviews
3. Observations
4. Document Analysis
5. Surveys

This blend of qualitative and quantitative approaches to gathering data are most commonly used processes among the 2%. However, they are tools that you too can use and apply to your own situation. Focus groups usually consist of 6-12 people and allows for uncensored, topic-driven discussion guided by a moderator. Interviews allow all players to share their perspective in a one-on-one trusted setting. Observations allow you to see both commendable and reckless behavior patterns. Document analysis is a silent approach to determining common themes within the organization's culture or climate. Lastly, surveys provide a numeric trend of thought patterns and perspectives.

The goal of scheduling an appointment with the problem is to *intentionally* seek resolution. Practices of early childhood educators center around intentional teaching, which requires the teacher to be purposeful and deliberate in their approach to nurturing the strengths of each child. This same intentionality is needed for the leader to effectively solve problems. Intentionally seeking implies that you will purposely allot time to address specific problems in order to gain specific and timely results.

Leadership Nugget: If you don't put it on your calendar, it will likely not happen. You have to schedule success in order to be successful.

SOLVE THE PROBLEM

Identify 3 dates when you will schedule time to intentionally seek resolution to the problem.

1.
2.
3.

Put these dates on your calendar and identify the approach(es) you will use to gather data (i.e., focus groups, interviews, etc.).

1.
2.
3.
4.
5.

Why is it important that you intentionally make an appointment to address the problem?

Step 3: Identify the Symptoms

You're still feeling a little under the weather, but you made it to the doctor's office. When you checked-in at the counter, the receptionist likely asked a bunch of questions related to your demographics. Is this still your physical address? Do you have a telephone number or email address that you'd like to update? Have you traveled out of the country within the last six weeks? Is your medical insurance active?

Once you respond to all of these questions, you're instructed to sit in the waiting room to answer more questions that are printed on documents attached to a clipboard. Do you have family history of diabetes, cancer, or high blood pressure? It seems that the moment you get to the end of the questionnaire, the nurse announces your name only to greet you with more questions. You finally make it to the cushioned bench in the examination room, after verifying your full name, DOB, and weight. Hereafter, the doctor probes the big question, as if you didn't explain it when you initially made the appointment, "What are you here for?"

Questions create a safe place for individuals to share how and what they feel. Leaders should never shy away from asking questions due to fear of receiving unwelcome answers. The symptoms of your problem are secretly wrapped in the answers to the questions you ask. It's easy to assume that your front-line team members had an astounding workday based on their productivity report. However, when asked the direct question, "How was your day?", the team members may share details that made their workday extremely stressful. A contentious working environment may help to explain the problem of poor retention or high turnover rates.

When you arrive at the doctor's office, you might not look as bad as you feel. But, that one question, "What are you here for," allows you to share what you didn't tell the receptionist or put on the forms you completed in the waiting room. Questions, questions, questions...and more questions help to identify the symptoms and enable the leader to diagnose the problem.

Whether you scheduled an appointment to have focus groups or conduct interviews, be sure to ask open-ended questions. These types of questions, rather than closed-ended questions, will help identify the symptoms that will nail down the problem.

Example:

Open-end Question:
If you were promoted to manager of the department, what would you do first?

Response to Open-end Question:
Allows the person to freely share their thoughts without restricting the response in any way.

Closed-end Question:
Once promoted, do you think the first thing a manager should do is meet with their team?

Response to Closed-end Question:
Forces a one-word response without explanation, and limits the ability to explain in greater detail the respondent's thoughts and feelings.

The key to identifying the symptoms to your problems is to create a space that allow individuals and groups to freely share their impressions. Leaders should practice listening without pronouncing obvious judgement in their body language or facial expressions. The more people talk, the greater chance the leader has of identifying the root cause of the existing problem.

Leadership Nugget: Healthy conversations lead to healthy solutions. Healthy solutions lead to resolved problems. The absence of problems makes room for positive results.

SOLVE THE PROBLEM

Choose one of the problems you listed in Step 1 on pg. 8.

Now, write an example of an open-ended question you might ask team members in order to identify the symptoms of the problem.

Write out the potential response to the question above.

If the answer is a one-word response, "yes" or "no", revise your question so that it is open-ended rather than closed-ended.

Write the revised question here:

Why is it important that you allow people to freely talk about the problem at hand?

Step 4: Give a Diagnosis

After surviving the large aggregation of questions presented to you, I'm sure you expected an intelligent response from the doctor. A doctor who's unhurried, normally pauses to consider the information you provided. Further, they repeat what you've shared in the effort to ensure that they understand your answers. If there are any gray areas, the doctor will likely ask more questions of you. Why? Because it's important to have as much information as possible before making a diagnosis.

The diagnosis explains the cause or interpretation of the perceived problem. It generally leads to the answer or solution to an enigmatic situation. In order to come as close as possible to an accurate diagnosis, it's important that the doctor considers all symptoms. Otherwise, the diagnosis is premature and without foundation. On its own, the naked eye cannot be trusted to render a proper diagnosis. A reliable diagnosis must consider facts that usually surface after probing, close examination, and lab tests.

Effective leaders should be careful not to impose personal bias when giving a diagnosis. It's easy to assume that someone has the stomach flu when you see them vomit. However, vomiting can also be a sign of motion sickness, a concussion, alcohol abuse, or even pregnancy for women.

How many times have you identified an obvious team member as the culprit, only to discover that it was an individual you least expected? When we superimpose our preconceived judgments before collecting all the facts, it takes much longer to reach the correct diagnosis. However, unbiased diagnosis shortens the distance between the problem and the solution as it forces the leader to consider the facts before identifying the winning ticket. Furthermore, you increase your chances of giving the right diagnosis the first time.

This step to problem-solving requires that you sharpen your decision-making skills. Most of the pressure leaders feel, is the result of constant, repeated demands for sound judgment. Good decisions usually yield good results; however, poor decisions are a sure path to unresolved problems marked by poor results.

Before giving a diagnosis of the problem, consider the following nuggets to help make a good decision:

1. Acknowledge that *you* need to make a decision.
2. Gather pertinent facts.
3. Qualify the facts as aggressive or passive.
4. Brainstorm possible solutions.
5. Choose the best alternative from the solutions presented.
6. Verbally share your decision with others.
7. Actively pursue the plan.

It's a good practice for leaders to delegate responsibilities and receive input from others, but when at the top of the hierarchy, they should never rely on team members to make decisions required of the highest-ranking personnel, YOU! The chief-of-staff must acknowledge the responsibility to gather the facts needed to make the right decision. Critical issues with aggressive facts, require imminent decisions, meaning that the leader doesn't have the liberty to wait years, months, or weeks as with passive facts. Rather, aggressive facts pressure the leader to make quick decisions, normally within days or hours.

After listing the facts available in the moment, brainstorm possible remedies to the problem and select the treatment that offers the best results. It's important that you verbally share your diagnosis of the problem and commit to pursuing a curative plan. Keeping your decision a secret, will only create an uncomfortable and insecure work environment and fail to keep the leader accountable.

Leadership Nugget: Symptoms inform the diagnosis. The diagnosis helps to identify the best solution to the problem.

SOLVE THE PROBLEM

Let's practice solving a problem you're dealing with or a hypothetical situation (you choose):

Why is it important that the primary leader make the decision in this matter?

What facts do you know about the current situation? These facts serve as symptoms to the problem. List as many as possible.

1.
2.
3.
4.
5.
6.
7.

Are these facts aggressive or passive?

Remember, aggressive facts need immediate attention; whereas, passive facts allow more time to decide.

1.
2.
3.
4.
5.
6.
7.

Based on the facts listed, what is your leader's diagnosis of the problem? *Example: low-morale, lack of teamwork, poor working environment, etc.*

What are possible solutions to solving the problem? List as many as you can think of.

Review your list of possible solutions and choose the best plan for productive results. Write your selection here:

Identify the team member(s) with whom you will verbally share your diagnosis and the decision that you've made.

Commit to providing and executing a solvent plan of action *(we will address how to write a POA in Step 5).*

Step 5: Prescribe the Plan

Can you imagine the doctor walking out of the room without giving you a plan of action for the fatal diagnosis? You're left with a plethora of emotions including fear, anger, confusion, and lots of unanswered questions. Even if the diagnosis is grim, you'd like to hear options that could lead to a possible turnaround. In the same way, your team members are looking for you to give them a plan, even in worst-case-scenarios.

The prescribed plan of action is absolutely essential to the resolution of the problem. If you don't tell the team what to do, they're left to seek answers using artificial resources rather than human resources. Artificial resources are less likely to be accurate as they will yield information from non-specific sources, which leave some with inaccurate information. Human resources are generally more accurate, because actual human efforts discover specific answers, that are proven by time and testing. This is not to totally discredit information provided by artificial resources, especially considering that there are some reputable virtual sites. Rather, to warn that if the leader doesn't provide answers by way of a written plan, team members are more apt to seek answers elsewhere and the remedy provided may not be specific to the diagnosis made. Further, the implementation of an artificial plan could jeopardize positive and authentic outcomes.

Recall the last time you received a prescription from the doctor. You likely listened to a verbal explanation of what the treatment would entail, followed by a written prescription that was either manually or electronically forwarded to the pharmacist. Without a written prescription, the pharmacist would refuse to prescribe any medication for treatment. A written plan, coupled with a verbal explanation, is necessary to solving the problem!

The written plan documents exactly what team members, or you, should do in order to work toward the resolution. It answers the questions, *"who, what, when, where, how, and why?"* Knowing who should perform specific task reduces the probability of experiencing role conflicts and organizational chaos. Carefully outlining the duties of team members provides an unquestionable roadmap to the end result. The documented timeframe notifies members, whether their duties should be executed daily, weekly, monthly, or annually. The location is key and advises who's privy to the information and details of the duties performed.

Be careful not to make the mistake of telling the team what to do without clear instructions on how to do it. We can feel overwhelmed when a medical doctor tells us to take an injection but doesn't offer instruction on how to use the syringe. Your team may have the necessary apparatus to perform the task but that doesn't negate the need for you to tell them how to properly use the tools. Finally, your why simply explains the expected outcome: "A daily aspirin may the lower the risk of a heart attack." Do you observe the trend here? Tell the team members what to do and explain the expected results from the efforts invested.

Let's not ignore the potential of side effects. Isn't it amazing how side effects are rarely discussed and are merely highlighted in small print on the prescription label or information sheet? Nevertheless, the fact that side effects are included in the plan denotes that the information should be read and thoughtfully considered. From this analogy, we can infer that a leader should have the ability to forecast and have a plan should any deviations arise.

Just as the medical staff instructs you to call 911 in the case of an emergency or to immediately contact your physician should any of the side effects occur, leaders should apprise team members of what to do if the plan of action goes awry. Murphy's Law states: "Anything that can go wrong will go wrong." While this may appear to be a pessimistic outlook, it's actually very optimistic because it plans for the best, even when confronted with the worst-case scenario.

Here are two benefits of a prescribed plan to the problem:

1. Allows for direct communication versus grape-vine communication.
2. Gives credence and authority to the instructions provided.

Grapevine communication is open to the subjectivity of the person giving instructions or telling the story. Whereas, direct communication is indisputable because it comes from the immediate leader by way of verbal or written details. When information is otherwise received, team members are able to weigh the content against the instructions given by the immediate leader and refute contradictions if necessary.

Have you ever noticed that the doctor's signature or endorsement is required on all prescriptions? Why? Because the signature confirms that this is the approved plan for the diagnosis. As you guide individuals and groups toward the solution to problems, be sure that your stamp of approval is apparent. This will ensure that team members are confident of their authority to carry out the written plan, whether you are physically present or not.

Leadership Nugget: People hear what you say but they're more apt to carry out the plan when they can read exactly what to do.

SOLVE THE PROBLEM

Let's prescribe the plan of action for the diagnosis you gave in Step 4:

Diagnosis:

Write a Summary of the Plan:

Who will be responsible for carrying out the plan (list all involved parties):

What will each team member be responsible for? List their specific assignments.

When do you expect specific tasks to be accomplished? Give specific dates whether short-term or long-term.

Where are the expected duties to be performed? Detail exact locations you expect your team member to report to.

How will your team members carry out the plan? What tools will you give them to be successful?

Briefly explain the expected outcome of specific tasks included in the plan. What is the expected end result of the prescribed plan?

Discuss additional details that you feel are important to share with your team.

Step 6: Schedule Follow-Ups

When there is a serious health condition, the doctor usually prescribes medication and informs the medical staff to schedule a follow-up appointment for you. Why? Because it's important for the doctor to observe how your body is responding to the treatment plan and prescription.

Moreover, you're expected to have an annual physical with your primary doctor. This is the recommended norm even if nothing is obviously wrong with your health. During the annual physical, the doctor is checking to determine whether your body is properly functioning and responding to the active demands of everyday life. Interestingly, you're able to make the next appointment 365 days in advance, prior to leaving the doctor's office.

If you're expected to have an annual check-up with no obvious signs of sickness and routine follow-ups when being treated for an illness, what makes you think that you can identify the symptoms, give a diagnosis, write a prescription, and walk away from the problem? You can't! It's imperative that you schedule follow-up meetings in order to check on the progress of the comprehensive plan and the team members who are working in tandem to help solve the problem.

Follow-up appointments can be similar to your initial appointment and adopt the same strategies used to gather data: (1) Focus Groups, (2) Interviews, (3) Observations, (4) Document Analysis, and (5) Surveys. The selected approach is often determined by whether you're managing a group or an individual. Also, whether you want the identity of the persons providing the data to remain anonymous or made known.

The intent of follow-up meetings mirrors the goal of longitudinal studies, which allows the researcher to observe and gather data over a period of time. The benefit of longitudinal studies is that you're able to observe patterns that were not initially identified. The observer is also able to gather details that might have been missed if there were no check-ins between the starting and finish time. Just the same, intentional follow-ups not only allow you to measure the team's progress but they give you the opportunity to discover additional details along the way that otherwise might remain unidentified.

Missing information is vital to solving the problem. If the patient isn't taking the prescribed medication, the doctor can't expect healing to be the end result. If the team isn't following the written plan, the leader shouldn't expect stellar outcomes. Awareness of activity, or lack thereof, will only happen if you deliberately schedule follow-up appointments and seek to obtain missing information. Failure to check in will further exacerbate an existing problem. For that reason, you shouldn't wait until the finale' to check on progress. Rather, peek in along the way to ensure that the end result is what you planned.

When scheduling follow-ups, consider operating in the mode of open systems rather than closed systems. Open systems encourage interaction with outside environments; whereas, closed systems operate without the involvement of outsiders. When team members encounter challenges, reassure them of the support you will provide outside of their immediate reach. No one should feel as if they have to turn inwardly in order to obtain all of the answers. Those who feel unsupported or chastised are less likely to share details with you, and your chances of obtaining the information needed to solve the problem, become even more remote.

The aim of a follow-up appointment is to help you reach your *GOAL* of solving the problem. Consider these action items when scheduling your follow-up:

1. **G**et a date that works for everybody.
2. **O**utline the expectations for the scheduled appointment.
3. **A**sk more questions to determine the progress made or lack thereof.
4. **L**isten to what the individual or group needs in order to feel supported.

If you're the only one sitting at the table, your meeting will be very unproductive. Therefore, you should select a date for the meeting that works for everyone involved. Inform the team members of the accomplishments you expect of the group and/or individuals at this point in the game. This will help your team prepare their progress reports, whether verbal or written, and will help you mark the location of success while on the journey toward solving the problem. When you get to the table, ask more questions. Remember, questions are the conduit to gaining information that helps to solve problems. You should take lots of notes before making your exit, then ask the team if there is anything they need from you, in order to succeed at their assigned tasks.

Leadership Nugget: Don't wait for the *plan* to crash. If you see it off course, schedule an appointment to reinforce the intended plan.

SOLVE THE PROBLEM

What is your target date to have the problem solved?

What date did you issue the plan of action to your team members?

Identify at minimum two dates that you will follow-up with your team.

Identify the setting you will use for each follow-meeting (i.e., teleconference, boardroom, interviews, etc.).

Have you informed everyone of the dates for the meeting? Did they agree to be there?

What progress do you expect to have at the scheduled meeting? Be sure to share this with team members prior to the follow-up.

Why are questions important in this setting?

What support will you give to your team members?

Step 7: Adjust the Prescription

Whew! You've done everything right so far; you acknowledged the problem, made an appointment, identified the symptoms, provided a diagnosis, prescribed the plan, and scheduled follow-up appointments. The problem at hand should shortly be solved or close to being rectified. But what happens when the problem persists or worsens?

Consider the response your doctor might have once it's determined that the prescribed medication is ineffective. It would be a disservice to stay with a plan that isn't working. Hence, the doctor will likely pause to reevaluate the diagnosis and prescription. Why? Because, there's a chance that the initial diagnosis is incorrect or the medication was not the best fit to address the issue.

You guessed it; the doctor has to admit the possibility of error in order to discover the best remedy. It doesn't mean that all efforts, until this point, are worthless. Rather, it implies that the facts presented should be reevaluated and reconsidered in search of a more effective plan.

It's never easy for leaders to admit they've made errors. The good news is that you don't have to do this when solving problems. The decision you made might prove to be unworkable in this situation, but that doesn't mean it's necessarily a poor decision. It could be a good solution to solve a different problem. When you decide that the plan isn't working, share with team members that because there were more possible reasons for the current issue, more time is needed to reevaluate, and determine the best course of action.

It's common to have a high level of confidence in the knowledge of medical doctors, but the truth is that they are simply practicing the study of medicine. As a leader who boldly confronts problems that need to be solved, you are practicing the execution of your leadership skills. In so doing, there's a chance that you will misdiagnose the problem. When this happens, you will have to start from the beginning of the problem-solving paradigm. Be careful not to discard the details you've collected so far, because, when coupled with additional details, they will be very helpful.

A misdiagnosis it not uncommon. How many people do you know who went to the doctor and were given medicine for a condition other than the one that really needed treatment? You're probably thinking that this is a sure case to sue the doctor. However, before you draw up the legal documents, know that malpractice only happens when the doctor **neglectfully** gives a diagnosis, **intentionally** delays a diagnosis, or **fails** to provide a diagnosis of the injury or ailment altogether. As a leader, you must safeguard your practice and organization from being guilty of such actions.

In order to do so, you should pay attention to outliers, which are simply less-noticeable variables that affect the interaction between the independent variable (cause/influence) and the dependent variable (effect/outcome). Symptoms guide you to the diagnosis, but perhaps it's possible that you didn't consider minor outliers because they weren't the obvious reasons for the problem.

Outliers are generally situated away or detached from the problem at hand. You might conclude that a team member prefers to always work alone rather than interacting with team members. On the surface, it appears that the person is isolated, territorial, or doesn't welcome input from others. However, this behavior could be caused by outliers that were missed in diagnosing the personality. Is it possible that the team member is fearful of rejection? Perhaps the person was bullied or harassed in a previous environment and as a result, shies away from groups. If you misdiagnose a person or situation, pause to consider the outliers as potential variables to the outcome you're experiencing.

Katz (1955) argued that leadership requires three basic skills; technical, human, and conceptual. Technical skills consider the leader's knowledge of a specific type of work or activity; human skills focus on the leader's ability to work with people; and conceptual skills focus on the leader's ability to work with ideas and concepts. The field of leadership will always require the interaction of people, and this exchange will determine the height of your influence.

Hence, it's important that you don't allow the technical and conceptual skills of leadership to override the human skillset needed. Focus on the people you serve because it's the people that help manifest the vision for the organization. Otherwise, you'll discover that it's very difficult to adjust the prescription, when you believe that people should just do the assigned work and agree with your ideas. This position will never yield the good outcomes you holistically desire as a model of influential leadership.

Adjust! Yes, this requires that you change the course of your original plan. Most leaders, whether they admit it or not, don't easily embrace change because it requires them to stretch outside their comfort zones. It's comfortable to keep giving the same strategy to the same team members. But it takes effort to reevaluate and adjust your strategy while shifting the roles of team members, if necessary.

As you prepare to adjust your plan of action, consider the inductive reasoning vs. deductive reasoning approach:

- Inductive Reasoning: Starts with a Conclusion
- Deductive Reasoning: Starts with a Premise

The previous diagnosis you made focused on the facts you gathered when you initially explored the symptoms of the problem. However, when there is an adverse effect to the prescribed plan, you must employ deductive reasoning. This opens another gateway to gather missed details while still considering the foundational premise you've already established. Whereas, inductive reasoning presents a closed thought-process and prevents possible outliers from penetrating the walls of the existing problem. Hence, the problem remains unsolved.

Never be afraid to write a new prescription after reevaluation. Once you've chartered your course, be sure to schedule follow-ups as with times past. This will help ensure that your current plan of action is the most suitable to solve the problem.

Leadership Nugget: Everything around you will inevitably change. If you don't intentionally change, you'll become obsolete.

SOLVE THE PROBLEM

What are the improvements you observe since you prescribed the first plan of action?

What are the challenges that still present as a problem?

What are the symptoms of the current challenges?

Identify potential outliers of the persisting problems.

What is your updated diagnosis based on the additional details gathered in the reevaluation?

What is the adjusted plan of action to solve the problem?

What is your modified target date to have the problem solved?

Identify at minimum two dates for follow-ups. These dates should be proportioned in timeframe considering your new target date.

Step 8: Make a Referral to the Specialist

Recall the last time you or someone you know had a chronic health problem that couldn't be addressed by your primary doctor. In this case, the primary doctor likely made a referral to a physician who specializes in that ailment. While all medical doctors have general knowledge regarding human anatomy, they also have a specialization in a particular field of study; i.e. cardiologist, brain surgeon, ENT, etc.

The referral made by the primary doctor isn't a sign of weakness, rather it's strong evidence of strength. Why? Because when the problem is solved, everybody wins. It doesn't matter who's responsible for the solution. What matters most is that the plan cures the problem.

Leaders should work together in order to discover the root of problems. When this happens, more helpful data emerges, which soon leads to a solution to the problem. Medical doctors generally make referrals to specialists within the same network. This suggests that leaders must be intentional to develop strategic partners with the ability and resources to solve problems beyond their own skillsets.

The power of a network is that the answer often lies within the group. One person may have the small detail needed to solve the problem you're encountering. You will often find that this is a give-and-take situation, when you have the answer that resolves another leader's issues.

Remaining isolated as a leader eventually becomes a disservice to you and your team. On the other hand, exposure increases the knowledge you have to share and execute winning strategies. Can you imagine the doctor forcing you to believe that the prescription provided will eventually bring healing, although you continue to have dangerous or painful side effects? Good leaders avoid this mistake by making timely referrals and allowing a specialist to provide intense treatment for the problem at hand.

Now, let's be honest. It is sometime difficult for a strong and powerful leader to admit that the team needs the input of another person. You don't have to confess; we'll do it for you, because most leaders have struggled with "power addiction" at one time or another. This happens when the leader can't release or share the tenets that come with leadership because of the lofty benefits they enjoy; i.e., being at the top of the hierarchy, financial gain, making big decisions, public celebration, and authority to reprimand. Some leaders are addicted and aware, while others are innocently unaware.

Here are a few questions that help to identify addictive leadership behaviors:

1. Are you always the smartest person in the room?
2. Are you there for the money or the mission?
3. Do you make decisions without consulting key team members?
4. Do you fail to acknowledge and celebrate the contributions of others?
5. Does highlighting issues and giving open correction of others make you feel good?

If you answered yes to any of these questions, it's likely that you're dealing with a power addiction that should be addressed immediately. After all, a person addicted to drugs doesn't have the wherewithal to guide someone else through treatment. Rather, it's imperative that they get clean in order to serve as a sponsor for others. The same is true for an egotistical leader who's in such a place of authority that it goes to their head.

The first step to treating dependent behavior is for the addict to verbally admit their weakness. You guessed it. The first step to regaining equilibrium is for the leader to admit, "I don't know." This is a simple acknowledgement that you don't have the solution to the current challenge. And more to the point, the help you need is currently more than you yourself can provide.

After you've put forth your best effort to solve a problem that seemingly won't resolve, it's important that you temporarily step away to reflect and determine who best can expand the treatment plan. When you identify this person, be prepared to share with them everything you've executed to that point. This is important because it will inform the specialist what has been done, or not, and assist with determining what to do next. It also demonstrates your ethical approach to leadership in that you have pursued the right actions to solve the problem.

Ethical leadership assumes that the leader seeks to do "right" in their conduct and character. It helps to determine whether the action taken was appropriate and honest. There are two common domains when considering ethical leadership:

>   <u>Utilitarianism</u>: Determines if the action taken produces the greater good for the people.
>
>   <u>Deontology:</u> Determines whether the action was taken out of duty or obligation, without considering its impact on the people you serve.

So, you haven't been able to solve the problem? Is it better to make a referral to a specialist, enabling the team to have a better outcome, or is it better to maintain your position as "the leader" and carry out your duties as usual? The most effective option is obvious: make a referral to the specialist.

Leadership Nugget: When you admit what you don't know, you position yourself to learn what you should know.

SOLVE THE PROBLEM

What is the problem that you can't seem to solve?

Identify individuals who specialize in treating that particular problem.

1.
2.
3.
4.
5.

Take a moment to identify other experts that can help solve categorical problems in the future. This will help build your leadership network.

1.
2.
3.
4.
5.

Considering the list of specialists, identify two that you'll contact and make a referral for the problem at hand.

1.
2.

Identify the date, by which you'll make the referral: _____

Do you think you took the right action by making a referral? Explain.

Conclusion

You've worked extremely hard to solve this problem. By now, the dilemma has been remedied using an action plan you provided or the problem is in the hands of a specialist for intense treatment. Whatever the case, take your lab coat off, have a seat, and rest.

Let us be the first to commend you for your commitment to the process of discovering the truth about solving problems!

The end result of research is the affirmation or development of new theoretical concepts. Theories are proposed explanations for existing phenomenon but are only derived by testing a hypothesis. A hypothesis is your proposition or assumption of the causal relationship between two entities.

You'll likely never hear rave reports about research that didn't yield a contributing theory to the field of research. However, it is not uncommon for a hypothesis to be unsupported after being tested.

For that reason, you should always feel accomplished as a leader when you put forth your greatest effort to solve problems. Whether the outcomes help to develop theory or not, it adds to existing literature that will guide another to discovering the truth.

In the beginning of our journey with you, we shared that scholars who make up the 2% of those with doctorate degrees graduated to this level after demonstrating their ability to apply research that helped to discover the truth. If your goal is to matriculate on this level, go for it! However, you should be confident that when disciplined to study, you have the same ability to unveil hidden details that will advance theory and inform practice.

It's easy for leaders to become burned out. When this happens, you should rest but never quit. Leadership is driven by the influence one has on a group or individuals. Can you imagine what would happen if you removed your positive impact from the process now? The problem might become worse and spiral downward, to include victimizing innocent followers in the process. Your influence is necessary to solving the problem.

Hence, we challenge you to revisit this 8-step process until the problem is solved:

- ⇒ Acknowledge the Problem
- ⇒ Make an Appointment
- ⇒ Identify the Symptoms
- ⇒ Give a Diagnosis
- ⇒ Prescribe the Plan
- ⇒ Schedule Follow-Ups
- ⇒ Adjust the Prescription
- ⇒ Make a Referral to the Specialist

Feel free to contact us with your results. We'd love to hear how you're adding to the rich field of leadership practice and theories.

About the Authors:

Dr. Darryl L. Grant

Darryl L. Grant is a graduate of Oral Roberts University in Tulsa, OK where he earned a BA in Theology and History, MA in Practical Theology, and D.Min. with a concentration in Church Ministries and Leadership. He is the Senior Pastor of Kingdom Builders Church International in Charlotte, NC where he leads a congregation of Christian believers who intentionally impact the community with love and deeds representative of Jesus Christ. He aims to always provide a doctrinal sound Word that increases the faith of believers and offers hope to others.

Mature in his approach to solving conflict, Dr. Grant is a mentor and counselor to leaders across cultural and denominational lines. His methodical leadership style is instrumental in assisting others with successfully yielding over and beyond intended outcomes.

Dr. Grant serves on numerous civic, community, and religious boards and committees, providing his resourceful leadership, acumen and experience. Most noted is his humility when engaging people of diverse socio-economic levels and his efforts to address the needs of the vulnerable.

Awards & Special Recognition

- The President's Volunteer Service Award (President Barack Obama)
- Top 100 Most Influential Pastors, Whole Truth Magazine COGIC
- North Carolina House of Representatives - Community Service Recognition (North Carolina 106th District – Mecklenburg County, State Representative Carla D. Cunningham)
- United States Congress - Community Service Recognition (North Carolina 12th District, United States Representative, Alma. S. Adams, Ph.D.)
- Beacon Light Award for Jurisdictional Superintendent of the Year

Website: www.kbcinc.org
Email: pastor@kbcinc.org

About the Authors:

DR. LAWANNE' S. GRANT

Lawanne' S. Grant earned a BS in Criminal Justice from Grambling State University graduating summa cum laude and salutatorian of her class. She advanced to obtain a MS in Administration of Criminal Justice from California State University, Sacramento, and a MA in Theology and Biblical Studies from Fuller Theological Seminary. She earned a Ph.D. in Business and Organizational Leadership conferred by Regent University. Dr. Lawanne' S. Grant is a Visiting Professor who teaches Leadership Organizational Behavior, Comparative Religions, and Philosophy classes.

Coupled with involvement in various outreach efforts, community programs, and professional organizations, Lawanne' S. Grant is a sought-after motivational speaker, mentor, and published author.

Dr. Grant served nearly fifteen years as a Deputy Probation Officer and has provided leadership coaching to religious and corporate leaders across the states for over twenty years. She is the founder and CEO of Leadership DevelopME, LLC with the mission of positively impacting the MIND and EXECUTION of leaders through coaching sessions, strategic planning, and book publications.

Awards & Special Recognition

- Woman of Influence Award, ACHI Magazine
- Top 150 Most Influential Women, Whole Truth Magazine COGIC
- Community Service Award, Association of Black Correctional Workers
- Featured Business Owner for Charlotte Business Resources

Website: www.leadershipdevelopme.com
Email: lgrant@leadershipdevelopme.com

References

Katz, R.L. (1955). Skills of an effective administrator. *Harvard Business Review, 33* (1), 33-42.

United States Census Bureau (2011). Retrieved from https://www.census.gov/.

Made in the USA
Monee, IL
16 January 2021

57812026R00046